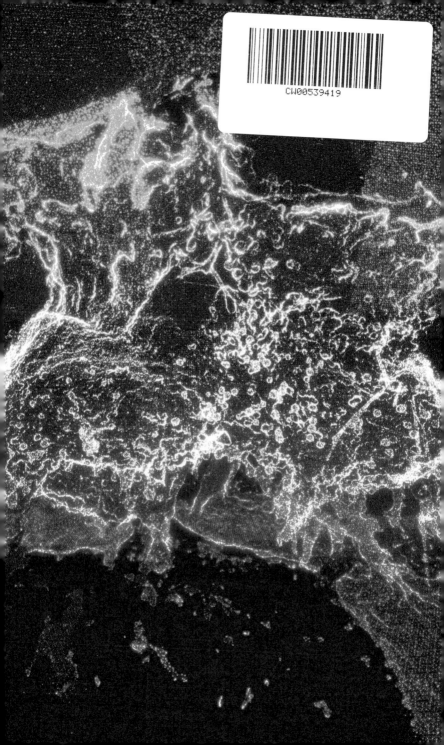

CW00539419

Altered States

Altered States

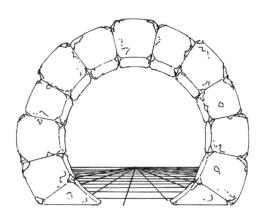

edited by
Sarah Shin and Ben Vickers

'Eruption from the Compound of Living' by Will Alexander, excerpted from *Refractive Africa: Ballet of the Forgotten* (Granta, 2022) is reproduced by permission of the publisher and the author.

'Initiation Notes: Journey of Compassion' by IONE, 23 June 1997, © IONE. A version of this text was first published in *Piramida Negra: A Live Letters Publication*, and is reproduced by permission of the author.

'undine cups' by Daisy Lafarge, originally commissioned by artist Mary Ramsden, is published by permission of the author.

A previous version of 'Carapace' by So Mayer was published (under the title 'Anthropocene') in *Visual Verse*, Vol. 6, Chapter 9, July 2019 and is reproduced by permission of the author.

'Solariuum: Light' by Irenosen Okojie, originally commissioned by the CCCB for the audiovisual project *Vocabulary For The Future* at the Kosmopolis Festival, is published by permission of the author.

'Dreams of the Sea' by Abd al-Ghani al-Nabulsi, translated by Yasmine Seale and published in *ArabLit Quarterly* ('Dreams', Winter 2020), is reproduced by permission of the translator.

'Pink Vendetta' by Mark von Schlegell excerpt from 'Charlene von Heyl: Piece By Piece' published in *Charline von Heyl: Paintings 1990-2010* (Les

Presses Du Reel, 2010) is reproduced by permission of the author.

'Entangled Life' by Merlin Sheldrake, words set to music by Cosmo Sheldrake.
First published by Ignota 2021
This selection © Ignota 2021
The contributions © the contributors 2021

1 3 5 7 9 10 8 6 4 2

Ignota
ignota.org

ISBN-13: 978-1-8380039-2-0

Design by Cecilia Serafini
Cover image by Jakob Kudsk Steensen, Berl-Berl, 2021: Undergrowth fungal network from the Spreewald, scanned with photogrammetry using a canoe
Typeset in Electra by Alice Spawls
Printed and bound in Great Britain by TJ Books Ltd

All rights reserved. No part of this publication may be reproduced, stored in a retrieval system or transmitted in any form or by any means, electronic, mechanical, photocopying, recording or otherwise, without prior permission in writing from Ignota Books.

The moral rights of the authors have been asserted.

Contents

Introduction

'You are the medicine.' María Sabina

Altered States opens out onto the lysergic tenebrosity of the twenty-first century. Tapping into orbits of transmission and reception, light and shadow, known and unknown, the poems gathered here explore varieties of consciousness and revelatory experience. Taken as a whole, *Altered States* is both the question and the process of seeking. What are altered states of consciousness? What defines alterity? Can altered states produce altered worlds?

Despite the frequent and reliable correlation of altered states to the ingestion of mind-altering substances, the majority of the poems in this volume speak more broadly to the mind-manifesting and revelatory meanings of the Greek roots of the word, *psychē* (ψυχή, 'mind', 'soul') and *dēloun* (δηλοῦν, 'to make visible', 'to reveal', 'to manifest'), enfolding the insights of psychoanalysis into the relationship between language and the unconscious.

This is a book of thresholds, where poetry forms the entrance to and the architecture of altered states – zones of experience that show the imbricated and simultaneous nature of realities whose connection is profound, but often obscure to the 'ordinary' conscious mind, which overlays what *is* with concepts and beliefs. Here, you may find something of the wild profusion of meaning emanating from the enigmatic interstices of our lives refracted into a seed, containing, to paraphrase Donna Haraway, a history of practices inside its coat[1]. This is a book of potential: for staying open, staying loose. For witnessing loss as it is happening around us, while recognising the emergent patterns of symbolic life as it floats downstream from heaven and hell and our nervous systems, and into our dreams.

Since the psychedelic experience has the structure of dreaming awake at the end of time – ungovernable, inviting diffusion and slanting articulations, and full of resemblances and chimeras – the question of how to tell the dream upon waking remains. And there is the perceiver of gestures and symbols, as full of meaning as they are constantly shifting: the dreamer, the voyager, who returns to tell about it. This, then, is a

i

book for you, offering glimpses through poetry of the other side in order
to show something of what *this* side might be: to allow for myth to fall
among the mundane and to find some medicine in the madness.

In collective consciousness, unveilings or turning points can be identif-
ied in cultures at points of coalescence and rupture, when knowledge is
born from complexity. As the introduction of coffee – the 'sober bever-
age' – to Europe became entwined with the rise of the Enlightenment,
the increasing legitimisation and industrialisation of psychedelic re-
search in the Western biomedical context suggests a coming paradigm
shift.[2] Public and scientific interest in psychedelic drugs has grown stead-
ily over much of the last two decades, with an exponential increase in
recent years backed by considerable investment. Clinical studies have
shown promising results for the use of mind-expanding drugs to treat
psychic distress by resetting pathways of pain, pleasure and behavioural
patterns, while many are exploring their benefits outside of the laboratory.

The current so-called 'third psychedelic renaissance', consecrated by
the scientific priesthood, presents an invitation to imagine a psychedelic
style for the twenty-first century. The world *as we know* it is a thing that
has become and is no longer becoming; an experimental trajectory into
the future means seizing the image of the past just as it becomes legible,
to perceive and reconstellate its forms. Language carries its culture on its
back, telling the story of its people and their episteme as it takes shape.
Altered States opens a space for sharing and making a language, a style, a
vibe. Poems by Jenna Sutela, Bhanu Kapil and Emily Segal play with
artificial intelligence and poetics to explore transformation, divination
and generation, while others articulate entanglement with other-than-
human ontologies, such as the 'merged becoming' of Rebecca Tamás'
'Echo: A Matriarch Engineered to Die', Merlin Sheldrake's mycelial
song, or Bett Williams and Rosemary Carroll's trip report, in which 'Bett
sees herself in a non-human form and understands that the lightning and
thunder that's been hanging around is not separate from Rosemary or
herself, but a part of them.'

Yet other poems, such as those by Yasmine Seale and Janaka Stucky,
continue eternal wanderings in the unbound and imaginal modes of
trance and dream, via Tai Shani's 'dreaming androids and the seraphim
who appear in flames' and James Goodwin's 'particle reach'. Catalysts for
altering states – or 'pivots in the world of resemblances', as Daisy Lafarge's
'undine cups' puts it – may include grief, plant allies, mushrooms, ritual,
psychoanalytic descent and journeys to temples of sound, while stylistic
and formal expressions of transmutation range from 'language as kinetic

distillation' in Will Alexander's multidimensional 'Eruption from the Compound of Living', instructions ('remold relations through you' directs Paige Emery in 'Instructions for Self-Hypnosis'), and 'the osmosis of hieroglyphs' in IONE's 'Initiation Notes: Journey of Compassion'.

The Mazatec *curandera* (healer) and visionary poet María Sabina, who first opened the *velada* mushroom ceremony to a Westerner in the 1950s, described the sacred mushrooms as speaking to her and giving her 'the perfect word', enabling her to 'cure with Language'.[3] This connection between language and healing – expressed in the *pharmakon*, meaning poison, remedy and sacrifice, as well as writing itself – is threaded through *Altered States*. Dorothea Lasky's 'The Chateau' is a spell that promises 'medicine for the entire world'; Hoa Nguyen's 'Roomy Poem Of No Mastery (Seven Times Three)' summons the 'mentor of medicine knowledge'; and Erica Scourti's 'Salty One' affirms 'the treatment is also the poison', while Johanna Hedva's 'What Doesn't Work' includes 'B e i n g p o i s o n e d b y t h e c u r e, b y l o v e'.

In the Western-dominated, de-ritualised twentieth century, the profane exploration of psychedelics often began with inadequate initiation and ended without integration, leaving the curative circuit incomplete, or elided entirely. In the broken chain of tradition, the altered state was mistaken for the final form, the representation for the treasure. But as a journey gains its meaning through return, the transformative potential of the altered state lies in the re-entry into 'ordinary' consciousness, since psychic topography is not of one origin and destination, but of many beginnings and many ends.

Experiences of altered states are often characterised by an enhanced quality of deep and implicit memory; the mushrooms, for Sabina, enabled her to 'arrive where the world was born'.[4] In this passage to the next epoch, the practice of integration – making new connections between the old and the previously unknown – offers the possibility of weaving alterity into the fabric of the everyday. Changing our worlds depends on changing ourselves through cultivating consciousness – to understand that integrating, like healing, or writing, is a process of remembering how to hold things in relation even as they are not quite commensurate, fractured and slipping away – so that every circumstance becomes an occasion for being otherwise. Medicine, in this light, means to remember the future, and it lies within you.

Sarah Shin and Ben Vickers
London, 23 October 2021 (Sun enters Scorpio)

[1] Donna J. Haraway, *Modest Witness@Second_Millenium.FemaleMan©_Meets_On coMouse™: Feminism and Technoscience* (New York and London: Routledge, 1997), (New York and London: Routledge, 1997), p.129

[2] 'The first coffeehouse in the West opened in Venice in 1560; from there, coffee spread north over the next century . . . Coffee was the new way: it resonated with images of distant places and foreign cultures; it was the spirit of the Enlightenment and supported the Enlightenment and was supported by it in turn.' Dale Pendell, *Pharmako/Dynamis: Stimulating Plants, Potions & Herbcraft*, (Berkeley, CA: North Atlantic Books, 2002), pp.21-23

[3] María Sabina, *Selections, edited by Jerome Rothenberg*, (Berkeley and Los Angeles, CA: University of California Press, 2003), p.25

[4] Sabina, p.29

Eruption from the Compound of Living
For Jean-Joseph Rabearivelo
Will Alexander

Beneath a luminous compound equator
inscribed on Madagascar
Jean-Joseph
you erupted from disquiet alive as post-zodiacal phantom
knowing from birth that your blood was none other than oneiric ferment

as the 'black glassmaker' *
you possessed invisible lingual beauty
having somehow risen above mange eaten wrath
& exposed its perjury by the mere fact of living

colonial wrath through refraction
singed your shadow through negation
lit a fire of riot in your system
tempestuously self-veiled from itself
via beatific blizzard
via inspiration as spiralling apogee
as trans-partisan inferno
striding through bedlam
via your living moment as insubstantial ash
as momentary doctrine

your roaming strewn with caliginous weaving
provoking useless gradients & doctrines
through which you strolled as cryptic leopard destined to dwell under
                                        the psychic cannibals of France

there was always this split inside you
this garrulous shading
this plague of contorted values
provoking in you peculiar lingual spells seminal with strychnine
certainly not a visibly wrecked mule
or a formless amalgam of rage
instead
intoxicated verbal power
aristocratic blazing

1

poetically sculpted telepathy
as terse invigorated agency

of course as phantom
as a-pragmatic migratory wanderer
you were eclectic with decimation
kinetically invisible
surrounded by mazes scattered with voids as interregnums
never sterile with domination
or with bitterness through terminal registration

spectral with navigation
you enunciated grace
via endemic lingual styling
not unlike compound telepathy enmeshed with magical laterality
being pluvial & involved in the midst of private colloquy
alive as imaginary irritant

as subtle germination
as ironic watery ash
filled with 'invisible rats'
with alchemic kindling from Imerina*
working via the kinesis of bravery equated with flashes that were glints
sans persistence as induction or forms of stabilized mirage

this being the stage of subtlety rendered antelope
a stage that implies mist where language empowers subconscious
                                                    formation
as prime symbol of otherness
as wind that erupts from sparkling emerald gulfs
from gazelles that wander through spinning solar habitation

this being language as kinetic distillation
& you
Jean-Joseph
continue to roam as otherness
as presence that squares itself with elements that raze & sunder carbon
as if our whole solar family had curiously slipped beyond existence itself

being 3/4 beyond our galactic mean
you found an entry point via prime tonality of your magical mental

scale
never as secular thought-wave
but as invisible oscillation where poetic syllabics glanced off of private
                                                    inner registration
so that magical glimmers protracted themselves

& as forms emerged from these glimmers
they furtively advanced beyond the post-exhaustive
sans decades & calculation

your language
implying dawn as magical realm
moving as apparition through apparition
so that there existed no eclipse from prior elements
that continued to spin & approximate calliope
so as to broker gulls from invisibility
so that you magically brokered the unseen
via verbal annealing
via solitude cleansed by momentary waking
via emptiness that rises above the state of universal bickering

& from the present plane we thank you
for aural power that weaves its way beyond what could be ironically
                                                    rendered static osmosis
that continues to mine nutrients from interstellar rotation
your writing sublimates power through seeming vacancy as non-effort
so that you never quite considered as colonized persona
but as strangely en-fired carbon
brought to bear as inflammatory riddle
Jean-Joseph
poet
gambler
spell chaser
collector of numerous female sirens *
seducing reality by inflammatory crystal
by phonemes spun from eclipse & fire

as if you counted sapphires in your sleep
yet all the while
forced to pose as a 5th rate caricature who characterized the French

with their stumbling & deception
that promised you transmission to Paris
so that you could have composed wave after wave of lingual oneirics
suffused by unsullied macaws & cobras
as magnificent declaration by Madagascar royalty
igniting subconscious states of indigenous cadastral power
always your language woven with the ubiquity of saffron

this was the Madagascar of the Hova *
with their self instilled panorama
with their fertility as living dossier un-invaded by tenebrous dimensional
                                                                    forces

understanding primeval declaration
you brought language to a glistening pitch
raising harmony to one of haunted illumination as it shone through
                                                            vitreous owls
rhyming with themselves
through strange galvanizing tenets
through alchemical swarming within themselves

such as the 'the Black glassmaker'
that continues to stun the mind as he surveys great orchids
prone to the tenor of impalpable neurons
allowing breath from other sums
from experiential hives
as something other than embellished stationary form
 the maze of your aural lens like a curious technical property
stunning
like aromatic tundra casting unseen formation

unlike protracted optical spell
or over-extended immersion evolved as recitation

being zeal as lingual inhalation
as magic mesmerism as insistence

scintillation that investigates its own fragility
all the while tensile with its curvature of tissue & moisture
that burns
that elliptically probes

4

beyond the realm of ashen cinder postings
that instigates transparency

for instance
I think of turquoise lemons that blaze as imminence
that cast themselves as dazzling lyrical motifs flowing through perfected
      grenadine monsoons as if they were stunning circadian anomalies
far beyond stasis as taut or personal writhing
or enjambment by prior circumference
but neutrality as the instantaneous
as a crazed portal with illuminated figures ascending from a yurt *
not as curious personas
or as beings that convey themselves as interchangeable substance
but as anterior to their own notion
seemingly transmuted into nouns
thus there exists no stasis
no problematical limit
primed by geriatric condensation
by wizened audacious claim studded by fractional constants

& so you
Jean-Joseph
blazing with interior specifics
with fiery osteology as chatter

you
being proliferation
were held from wider view
withheld from frames of view in Amsterdam & London
withheld from verbal view
until noted by Senghor *
over-coming the abject powers that circuitous withheld you
that always embrangled momentum
that stratified poetic emission by assembling consternation
as result
your vertiginous grappling torrent
its circuitous hull cracked open & made episodic with riddles
that circumvented daring
bringing your lovers into judgment concerning alien hypocrisy & its
claims
that measured their worth according to banal respectability

according to their stance as colonial lepers
according to their adaptation of realms that functioned through
                                        carnivorous containment

as garrulous renegado seemingly scrambled
you remained magically calm & reflective at the core
living on a plane of contradictory omens
not unlike an occulted prince conjuring principles from opaque
                                        investiture
concerning salience as poetic ensemble
as beatific conundrum
concerning traces that extended beyond all five palpable senses . . .

The World
K Allado-McDowell

Deep inside yourself, beneath the shuttling transport of the conscious
mind, there is a vast black tube of sky, which you fall through. At the
bottom of the fall lies a cold obsidian lake. Its surface is perfect and
unperturbed. You pass into it, like a ghost passes through a wall.

There is pressure here, pressure on the lungs and the skin. Tender flesh
rips at your neck as gills slit open. You inhale deeply and cough,
exhaling the last of your air, which dissolves in a thousand tiny worlds.

You sink down. You slow. Your feet touch rough stone – the bottom of
the lake. Under the sole of your left foot a small ache becomes a
stabbing then an ejection and a release. You bend down to pick up a
pebble.

In the darkness you see nothing. Yet the pebble radiates visible
emptiness. You hold it up to one eye. This is what you perceive:

A haggard caravan trudging through a desert.

A wall that extends for hundreds of miles.

The sneering face of the child who bullied you.

Engineers before computers, their minds running in loops.

You hear the patter of rain on stone. You smell petrichor swirling in
vines. You reach down to stroke your child's soft skin. On your wrist
is a golden bracelet.
You snap in the leather seat, twisting to face your spouse. The
freeway is a symphony. The windows go dark.

The walls of your cage tremble. The door wrenches open. A
balaclavaed face – run!

A stinging tincture of belladonna dissolves on your tongue. Baroque
harmonies vibrate the air, unfurling. Your neck rolls back and
loosens your gaze. Angels hover high in the cathedral.

Machete in hand, you sweat and hack at sugar cane, beneath a blazing sun.

You pull the brown hood over your head. Potent light streams through glass stained in red, piercing blue, burning yellow, a flower of life, air cold with dust.

Everything smells like green tea. You run the customer's credit card. A migraine is coming.

You dig through a box of receipts and pay stubs. You remember breaking your arm. Your partner grew weary of your need for help. You had to learn how to wipe with your left hand. Painkillers messed with your memory.

You woke one day and five chicks had died, their feet caught in wire too close to the heat lamp. It's part of farm life but you're not a farmer. You were just house-sitting. Death seemed to follow you around that house.

You're falling asleep in your best friend's sweater. Your flight leaves at 7 a.m.

A flood washed away the house and the two cows.

You taught the machine to sing. No one liked the way it sounded. You published the paper anyway.

You were chopping celery to make soup and you wanted to cry because you felt trapped.

You remembered your first breath of air. You tried to write down what it tasted like but the words escaped.

You swim toward light and the surface. A point pierces the water, screaming through your spine and gills. A rock crushes your skull.

You are walking down a familiar street, the one that takes you home. Your calves are sore from running. You count the final steps. Your hands are stiff. Your mind is a barren landscape, a simple cover for an exhausted body. You're hungry. There is food for you. A guest, a secret lover, cooks in your kitchen. They greet you with a strong shoulder, with fingers that run through your unwashed hair and massage the knots in your scalp. You relax into their structure.

'Shower,' you say. 'I need a shower.'

You smell cumin toasting in oil. Steam finds its way from the kitchen, bringing turmeric and frying onion, peppers, the singe of plants on hot metal, the graceful fragrance of rice. You climb the stairs to your bedroom. You can't remember waking this morning. It was decades ago. Someone else made the bed. Cool linen beckons.

You unzip your uniform, starting at the crown of your head. Your zipper is a line of light. You draw it over your forehead, feeling fluid release as your uniform parts in two. It drips down your face and over your eyes. It is warm, the temperature of blood, but its taste is milk, honey and salt. You wait to feel the ambient heat, to see the steam. Then you dive in. You are drenched in the flow. Moving liquid wraps your body like a ribbon, an ouroboros.

This is *The World*.

You rise to the peak of a Ferris wheel. Feel yourself freed from gravity. Cresting the wheel, your body is filled with light. You are cleansed. Naked, you are complete. You have become what you set out to be. Your mind is a diamond. You are light.

Then . . .

A downward rush and the perfect force of gravity. Matter rolls you under, pulling you forward again. The void is a moment drawn behind you. A future appears to take its place. A hunger, made within you, is growing within you. Across a distance neither time nor space, your consort's touch awaits.

From *God Complex*
Rachael Allen

It's a risk, a life with someone. I can remember the last time we saw
each other as incompatible lovers. You were standing in the doorway
with a rucksack made for camping, holding most of your belongings. I
felt a shift occur in my body, as when the impossible happens, unnatu-
rally, a deviation and then a decision towards a new reality. The blood
switches direction in the vein. What dictates that blood should always
pulse one way and not the other? That someone should leave or stay? I
felt the passing of time and era move through me as I have felt the
physical shift of sea turn to induce a bad tide, a deeper and colder water
coming, an underlying tugging into open ocean.

It was low burrs of late July humming light, aging sun, pollen gore.
When I watched you go it was as though at a distance. I thought – I am
seeing you leave for the final time – impressing and falsifying the
sincerity of the scene. The light behind you halo-made your head and it
was cliché. I wouldn't see you again.

How to tell a story faithfully and to the cause? We had lived by a river, a black water garden. Red roots grew from the banks like a picture I remember of a Monsanto-plumped lake, making everything turn pink when I swam in it. Our river was deep and ran according to my moods. I know this because, as a child, I controlled the sea. I stood at the shore and, hiding from my mother, with my mind, would command the waves to move in certain ways: Octopus-like, babbling brook, raging storm. I didn't tell a soul for fear I might lose the power, but I did tell you.

When things were better, we'd walk the river. In the summer, stop by a bar and have a cool drink. Sometimes there were bars on the river, sometimes the bars were closed up. Once, twice, three times a year, the river would burst its bank. The river would burst its muscly banks all over the closed bars and into our house, dark, like someone in an unpredictable rage.

I stood where we first met and was inconsolable. Crazed moon options followed me in the sky like a portent. Coastal grains, solar noon. I would ask: are you done with me? Fly in the buttercream of a plastic rose. The river is moving too quickly and the bloated strands of it all at once. The river and the wires above it shaking like a fit, that perfectly matched my mood.

For a while I had this catastrophic resistance to other people that comes after a great saturation of feeling, an adrenal failure. I'm leaving Europe while the clouds look British. History just goes binge purge binge purge like me and like me its heart busted by the river. I was knackered. As knackered as the Madonna della Misericordia, holding all the men.

Grief is built to practice alone. Like sexual deviance. The theatre of its being is vast, lonely and without share. It is a house imposing, slanted on a hill, like in a painting, one rusty bucket burning on the incline. Manipulative and symbolic, like a film, even to talk about it like this proves all this in grief is performance. Tada.

I stayed in the city by the river for a while after you left, it failed me. I knew I still lived in the thick of the separation that moved through my body like that rough, unfamiliar blood. It altered a chemical balance. The heartache cannibalised, and I was distracted to the point of mental absence. I lived tethered so intensely to a present moment I lost all interest in my body's physical needs. I had memory loss in its extreme, which adapted, became futuristic, so much so that I could not comprehend a time that I would one day even need to try and remember, so I stopped preparing for one. I was readying myself for un-memory. I became filth and never stopped fiddling with my pants. The taps stopped working in my house and I didn't let the landlord know. The building fell into disarray and a slim, vibrant green vine grew from the damp of the skirting board. It was making its way towards me, it wanted to bind up around my frame, which rarely moved. I removed myself from everything and became inverted.

Sun-wrecked, river slapped, useless miscellaneous. Describe the brown: I wanted a life I knew I was not accessing. I'd think: it lives at the bottom of this river. There is not control at any point in a narrative. Breeding swans on the bank. I despised the lone mother bird for her freedom, weighted down by felt grey babies with no consideration for what she can afford. The swan is a bitch. I took that from a book. One soft cygnet pokes innocent up through white feathers, like in a Rococo painting, eyelash-tacky and colour swept; poverty begets, and has this long memory, a memory stretching over me still, a sunset curdling and on pause. You are made a different colour in poverty; it is visible to everyone. In animals you do not see it.

Moth beaten. Gorge on earth, when we are very hungry, or at least when starved of a very true romance. A romance that is as untrustworthy as a dune and scatters like a dune in even a faint wind. Glass against the wall is not an indication of an occurrence of nature or what is natural. Steam engine furiosity and break. Don't ask me to explain empty stomach / emergency cigarette, or walking through the motions of passing through an old house that you inhabited with a heartbreak so epic it could end climate. Days you could not lift a spoon to your mouth. Another day would always follow it.

I cannot compete if we are the same species. Sitting on stoup in the most gothic of autumn. A phone in my hand and a cajoling through it, giving over poor news to my contacts like a bad TV. Reach up and shut it off.

Caterpillar gnostic face, the outside world is infected and has been so since we took off apart.

I watched myself perform as though televised watched the great ice shelf sink into the blue abyss learned about the paradise crow on the History Channel cartooned inaccurate drawings led to years of misinformation.

I will be believed one day, if not for this performance then perhaps my next. What would happen if there was a microphone installed somewhere in this bedroom? Yes I too cannot remember what we ever talked about.

(before firewood prays, she hears)
Khairani Barokka

a burning woman makes a shitty comrade
the smoke's cumbersome, fire a safety hazard

so what if the firemen gagged her with a gasoline rag, so—
they slit her with a lighter and threatened any decibels

on the arboreal gurney. enough times of facing angry shouts
for screaming, the sapling lost the ability to verbalise flames
'appropriately'

for branches to remain 'appropriate' requires time's reversal
and denial of how often she bursts into the maw of a star

why go back and back there, for kicks?
why spread an inferno to flooding steppes

black clouds look like breath, her knifing chest
no longer understands a divide of sky and flames

tug an ash braid. see if it's god in there,
the one her mother said lives inside her with the blades

dust sucker
Jen Calleja

Dustsceawung (Old English): contemplation of the fact that dust used
to be other things – the walls of a city, the chief of the guards, a book, a
great tree: dust is always the ultimate destination. Such contemplation
may loosen the grip of our worldly desires. – 'Untranslatable Words,'
The School of Life

I am a sand castle of a woman

*

if I breathe too much exhaust it will lodge in my lungs
and bear a grudge

I feel like I'm walking along the curb of a busy road, coughing
eyes running

I need a good thump
like thrashing a rug after winter

*

for too long
woodland and forests have been seen
as the side salad to the steak
the crust on the jam/ham sandwich
somehow: the past

they were eternity all along

a zillion specks
no beginning no end
camouflage correlated
in dialogue
over millennia

*

the tread of my shoe is a display case
cradling a fragment from
my daily meandering

I have a display case of mud clots slowly crumbling

I wake in the night and calmly think: is that a blood clot
gently rumbling

*

dusting for fingerprints
chalky white over everything
like a tick
suckling the juice, rotten little sucker!
leaving your mark
like a snail trailing over books
it didn't write

*

cocoa on a cappuccino in the shape of a toad

the cat comes in sparkling with pollen and seeds

*

my desk is piled high with
charcoal dust

it trickles from between covers
into the covers of my bed

I spend my time sieving it, moving it from
one bucket to another

*

I'd rather sleep on a public beach
than in my bed

the dusty feeling on my hands afterwards
from handling salty stones and shells
like after hoovering up a dish of pistachios

*

white plastic bags of
reasonably priced fruit, günstiges obst,
wash off the rough film of pesticide
dusty scent of a peach tickling my throat

*

when my friend knows I'm leaving
they start hoovering and won't stop till I'm gone.

my friends,
mycelium

*

german feels chewy and sweet on my tongue,
not flaky, not like choking-hazard-english

I roll maltese around in my mouth like an everlasting gobstopper
that gets no smaller, no matter how much
I suck

my dad won't put his bil-malti teeth in anymore,
my mum mimics her irish ma only never

*

in spite of everything, my parents' air
fizzes and froths with laughter

so why, in spite of not much,
are we two submerged in CO_2 sighs?

*

I've got names gathering dust in a folder on my phone

you can always adopt
like adding hot water to granules
but it ain't all gravy

the website depicts adoption as a winding asphalt road
all sleeping policemen and no rise-and-shine bumps

you can always adapt

*

I'm the diplomat between my lover and my body
but no interpreters are ever available

when it's time for that famous intimacy
I'm always constricted in a musty latex catsuit from the eighties
and the zip is jammed

I think I can proceed but then
a flea bites me on the ankle
dust bunnies tumbleweed under the bed

the bunnies and the flea are of the opinion
that I should just close my eyes

you'll see

Circuits
Jesse Darling

The fair smells like pork grease & donuts, neons
bright in the rain. A drunk I went to school with
rides the ghost train alone. I go in my pocket for coins
& there's the lucky stone been weighing down my coat;
don't know who gave it me or why, but its heavy
as any other blessing. Today they took so much blood,
a long list of tests to discover how good I could be
at giving or having life, & on the list it clearly said:
NOT DECEASED. Do u have everything u need she goes,
sex? Coffee? I'm like, if u got it? A large look passed between us
                    & then. I told her of the glory
of dreaming aloud & the long moments, sometimes days,
before it becomes terrifying. Wild flight, communion – & meanwhile
in here it's all awkward smiles & half entendres, as sickly
but bright-eyed I take my inevitable leave.

A Ouija boredom puppets up the old ghosts
& machinery until it's all whirring out there
in the were-world, murmuring & yammering hum.
& the ghosts sing *whooooo,*
                    weeeeeeeeee,
                            ussssssssss!? !   ?

            & the punchline
            clicks!
into! place!

Instructions for Self-Hypnosis
Paige Emery

Settle into a comfortable position.
Take long, slow, breaths.
  Inhale, relax your eyelids
    Exhale, close your eyes
      Inhale, open rest here
        Exhale, close your eyes
          Inhale, open warm rest
        Exhale, close your eyes
      Inhale, open thick warmth
    Exhale, heavy eyes
      (It's ok if you are tired)
        gentle thick
          dripping weight
            dripping down
              your cheeks honey
            your lips lavender
          your neck softens
      your shoulders sedate
  your back melts
   your hips sink
     your legs release
       your feet feathers
         One deep sleep
        Two deep sleep
       Three deep sleep
        Four deep sleep
       Five deep sleep

You stand here at top of the staircase
look down the
steps descend
you descend with
the steps down
>*Twenty see down*
>*Nineteen breathe down*
>>*Eighteen free down*
>>>*Seventeen down*
>>>*Sixteen lean down*
>>>*Fifteen breeze down*
>>>*Fourteen breathe down*
>>>>*Thirteen feel down*
>>>>*Twelve feeling down*
>>>>*Eleven ease down*
>>>>*Ten release down*
>>>>>*Nine relief down*
>>>>>*Eight beneath down*
>>>>>*Seven sink down*
>>>>>*Six seeping down*
>>>>>*Five deeper down*
>>>>>*Four deeper down*
>>>>>*Three deeper down*
>>>>>*Two deeper down*
>>>>>*One deeper down*
>>>>>*Zero you lay in the most comforting place*

D i s s o l v e

Liquescent   you   effervescent

your body floats in water   seeping body

within water   water within seep body blue   floating in

gentle water   safe sapphire water   soothing sky hovers blue

cool breeze weaves with warm night aroma soothesblue moonlight serene

lily pads lay cattails whisper along edges   willows wisp   hushes sway

gentle ripples   on fingertips pull   formless body fluid   foaming body

settles rebirth waves become you Press together finger and thumb firm and

speak yourself words you need to hear floating you can be words to appear

'I *have a choice.*   I *have a choice.*   I have a choice.'*

write yourself into form like song   *Press. Say.*   Betweeness shapes

like sing   *Press. Say.*   pearl-light illuminates your words

back to you   *Press. Say.*   remold relations through you

Press. Say.   Linger here   linger longer than

you think   *Press. Say.*   truth   With

f e e l i n g

One   you are in a body
Two   sense your tingling body
Three   shimmers with surroundings
Four   body reborn in the world
Five   wide awake wide awake!

*At any moment hereon, press together your finger and thumb firmly while repeating your healing words to remember. Your body remembers the more you repeat.

PARTICLE REACH
James Goodwin

resonance stretched out particle reach of all paucity meets
our sounding pulse and range. crystal lattice enfleshed in
earth or air like hem we trance. rings through first day's
sky on a black bird clapping tone light, seen bending the
same moon we eavesdrop drip black bone. waited left
hearing plying clusters of hum and hex crowing a
particle glaze windswept caught on bell rock's ocean spread,
off-white verve, diamond-cut overghost/ its hydroptic spine
crangs a mineral crest and rise 'flecting glints of a duppy's
passing iridescence gleaned under stream's lysed black lit
glow /on road/ glossed lowly. our pull up in the
darkness more spectral jaunt with the spectral wisp/ sweet
ethereal set back away rolling back, loose sway and
swing, cross fly hollow leap in-out like conch shell horn

After Bewilderment
Hannah Gregory

Q – the Quidam, the unknown one – or I, is turning in a circle and keeps passing herself on her way around, her former self, her later self, and the trace of this passage is marked by a rhyme, a coded message for 'I have been here before, I will return.'

At the light ecstatic time of year, swallows spiral in the space between hof and sky, their wings attached as brackets against yellow and pink, backlit. Muted in the present wake, washed out with loss. Corkscrews in the rectangular chamber, stirring air.

You need to dive,
and then you need to surface

The unconscious versus
the heliacal rise of Sirius

For an insomniac I,
swallows long-settled in some nest,
this window must be thrown open
to rain.

The TV tower's red glow
flashes a patch of cloud amber;
inverse ambulance lights
reflect blue off buildings.

The psyche is a weather system.
The error of pathetic fallacy reads
emotional turbulence:

                      landslides.

Deep missing
in the stomach's cavity
in the ground after a storm.

Welcome the deluge at the end of the canicule
(heatwave, *dies caniculares*, dog days)
that capsizes mood.

Earlier, soft rain steadily falling outside another open window, sotto voce approximating the mother more than the father, or – the ideal – neither. Surrogate parent or none, *a parent* or *apparent* – there are plusses to being not-real, to just being there.

Quidam: the unknown one, a character unnamed, a placeholder of a person.

I would like to cry, but crying interrupts saying, and the prerogative here is to say. I start to say then stop because I would like to cry.

I say: I think the demand is
                    [love].

This demand has taken more than one hundred hours of being in the room to come.

Having spoken the demand, without really making it, for its enunciation comes with a delay, I feel ready to leave, to be let go, and announce this.

                    How come?
                    'Love' – run.

When it's time, the rain is incessant:
no need to go swimming today.

The 'there' (of 'you') is both the ocean and the state

I dreamed the ocean
– but not before a series of narrow bureaucratic corridors
I walk down, following, until you disappear.
Through which door I do not know.
The longest corridor opens out onto the white-washed roof terrace of a
Grecian edifice, overlooking sea.
In the distance, a foreboding fortress.
I sense you are not in the fortress –

language-container
save us
from limitlessness.

I sense you did not go out to sea. I consider climbing down, swimming out
into slate water, but instead turn back inside,
beckoning appointments, patrolling officers,
all these murmurings caught like bees in unwashed hair.

I don't want to drown
in the mother ocean
mouth, which suffocates
as much as soothes.

I don't want to be returned.

Still can't find you.

all layers of 'I' interchange, revolving in an endless unsettling …

I dream the ocean – the bracing ocean of your maternal home. We're
wading out into the water, silvered light, with you ahead,
as you would be in waking life, less hesitant than me,
more tentative behind, turning and wondering
how wet I should get how wet I should get with you.

Weathering the losses means at once
                              stepping into pools of grief
                  and lifting yourself
                                      two taut arms
                                      out again.

Or, to emerge
like a dog in slow motion
shaking one's coat dry.

The threshold may not only be between present and regressive selves,
but between species of feeling.

The unconscious versus
the cyclic time of us

After the birds dive,
they ascend.

Sources

Quidam – Fanny Howe, 'Bewilderment' | Diving, submerging, re-emerging – Marion Milner's description of an 'oscillation between states', as told by Jackie Wang in her lecture 'Oceanic Feeling and Communist Affect' | The ocean and the state – Jackie Wang | The question of a link between *a parent* and *apparent* – Fred Moten, *All That Beauty* | The revolving 'I' – adapted from Trinh T. Minh-ha, *Woman, Native, Other*, section, 'Infinite Layers: I am not i can be you and me' | 'Weathering the losses' – Alex Colston, 'Eros After Covid' | With thanks to Lizzie Homersham for the compressions and Edwina Attlee for the eye.

What Doesn't Work
Johanna Hedva

Drugs   Being in the body   Forgetting the body   Em
bodying the body   Getting out of the body   Getting
rid of the body   Getting the body back   God's hoove
s on my back   Opennesses   Thunderstorms that don
't stop   Decoding Gödel's Uncertainty   Deep breat
hing   Swallowing pills   Eating the dark   Sucking o
n the light   Needing   Asking   Spooky action at a di
stance   The toolessness of childhood   The little do
me of our love   Breaching   The knife, the needle, the
bread you try to form   The claustrophobia of being i
n hell without a thesaurus   The tedious calculus of
six sessions of Cognitive Behavioral Therapy paid fo
r by the insurance company   Autoeroticasphyxiatio
n   When my mother hit me and I spent the rest of my
life defending myself   Getting bad tattoos while hig
h   The lamp of passion that leads you in deep then le
aves you there in the dark   Spending all your money
to get to the ocean   A great interior architecture th
at none can know   Feeling the sedative start to bran
ch in you   Taking the skin off   Plugging in to nothi
ng electric   Banishing the unwanted   Cursing what
's invaded   Running — to, away, nowhere, home   Bei
ng poisoned by the cure, by love   Starving the tumo
r but feeding the sick   The key I found to the door wi
th no lock   All that fucking care that came unbidden
All the care that didn't

Oil Wheel
Caspar Heinemann

whatever next, i dig myself a fancy hole to leak
outing the debris of the dreamscape, training
myself to stretch to accommodate nurturing,
punishment, the return of the steam engine, the audience
of one with eternity gone wild, again

this hypothesis gets all rash and stolen, flustered
amongst the hive a thousand heavens linger bow-legged,
tetchy, hard-won, stung between the citadel and the carpal tunnel
what they don't want you to know, is, as an expert witness,
we all get all the milk for free all the time

cos it's a knowledge that makes you – well,
it makes me, you know, receptive, in a way i'm into
the aerospace project distilled to apple blossom
candied tongue on the dome of the aquarium
real fake fur chomping at the bit for the bloody roadkill

and so, i call upon my army of anoraks,
scat upon fortean times, ghost-heavy, creepy, ready
for elbow deep in the wyrd and wonderful world of financial
crime in the truest sense,
now, syndicated, balanced

across the spiky rafter of the world, hawking my cosmology, i am not
an incorporated company, not my own associate, not my own
arsehole – heaven rejects a man with a plan, abandon that worldly
shit on the world, and so the silkworms spin the lifeway for tuppence
eternity in the upside down hospital fountain

Initiation Notes: Journey of Compassion
IONE

There is a deep longing that travels with me always. Longing for the scented land of Egypt – West bank of Aswan – Golden shores.

Processing this Journey of Compassion – Egypt Again. I cannot express how happy I am to be returning. Always returning.

Anne is writing about some of what we discovered in the temples related to sound.

I was hearing it, but not yet understanding it – starting with first being in the Sarcophagus.

The sound amplifies, but in an extraordinary way.

In the Great Pyramid high up in the 'King's Chamber' the candle went out as we stood in a circle, sounding the directions. Then, in the comforting dark, we could really experience being there.

It was in the North that I realised that I was seeing tiny constellations in the ceiling. They were floating above us. I had the feeling they were always there.

They emerged in response to sound in the North. Were they showing ancient North Star positions?

I blinked and looked again. They were still there.

Many heard and felt the presence of other beings, close by in the dark.

It was at Karnak that I realised the depth of it all in the Sound Temple – the one with the unusual double ceiling (copper?) – there, the other voices seemed to be joining in with us. We also felt drawn to move in certain ways.

This has been happening before – it was on the island of Philae that the stories began to come through. Here, the Memories came in on sound:

INITIATION:

The Nubian guide I've known forever has taken my hand. His – large and soft and dry, encompassing mine, leading me here to safety. Temple birds are singing full-throated as we white birds gather inside.

I am melting against the walls, letting the stone cushion and cradle me.

Pressing the hieroglyph for Energy – for Water –

I bring a message for each:

It is the willingness to be perfectly in the moment.

And then there's the ability to be open.

While being perfectly in the moment.

One or more people who do this can do it for others.

There is the osmosis of hieroglyphs, meaning seeping in.

They are sacred!

Magical in themselves.

We are being worked by their magic. More and more as we open to it.

Keep recreating it.

Keep tracking it.

Holding the space/authority, the temple recreates itself.

The priestesses are still here with us.

All that is happening now, is known in the past.

Hotep!

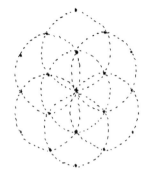

'Particles of Sound' by Anne Bourne

Killing a Word
Lucy Ives

Although the title of this exercise sounds a bit violent, it is actually a fairly contemplative undertaking. If one repeats a word enough times it may 'die.' Walk around one day and experiment with repeating a word over and over until it stops making sense. Type it 25 times. Write a poem in which you cause one or more words to die through incessant repetition. See what sort of effect this creates. Some words die hard. Some die rather easily.

A word like 'new' is easy to kill. Write it once at the top of a page and already it is unclear how these strange three letters can add up to such a significant and useful concept! However, a word like 'promiscuous' will die much less easily. It may take some repeating and questioning and doing to cause such a word to lose its meaning.

Emerson (not always my favorite) has anecdote about his own experience of the death of words in one of his journals:

> I remember when a child in the pew on Sundays amusing myself with saying over common words as 'black,' 'white,' 'board,' &c twenty or thirty times, until the word lost all meaning & fixedness, & I began to doubt which was the right name for the thing, when I saw that neither had any natural relation, but were all arbitrary.

What is it we're left with once a word has died? What is that strange sound or orthographic unit, that stub or deflated container? A poem that is the occasion of the death of a word might be something like an anatomy of that word – or, perhaps, an elegy. Gertrude Stein, for one, excelled at bringing about the deaths of words, as well as their reanimation and re-imbuement with life. This exercise can be the basis for many kinds of writing.

AI Owl
Bhanu Kapil

for Alycia Pirmohamed

Intimate and broad, the AI owl is spectre + oblong. Zoom fails but the
AI owl transmits each sneer or wobble. 'Can you hear what she's
saying?' – Midge, to whom? I'm reading poems in an indoor setting for
the first time since the pandemic began. Mesh-mouthed, the AI owl has
no beak.

'Bhanu, did you know that when the Phoenix lands on the lotus, each
petal releases a drop of golden water. If that drop falls off the flower and
into the water, and if a fish drinks that golden droplet, it turns into a
pearl?' No. This is gullet time. I'm up for it, Uluu. Urdu for owl, my
mother's childhood name.

Is this a portal? I've come to associate owls with sources of light,
invented pathways in the work. What feels possible, or less possible
now? The owl's hoot makes a link between what never belonged to us
and the feeling of radical gain that was a hallmark of our century. Says
nobody. What's wrong?

Behind the AI owl is a moon. Behind the moon is a rose. In this
equation, the one you long to meet is drinking tea at 7 a.m. Invert the
drawing, and there's an owl, shabby-brown in the plaza. With a flourish,
I scoff my tart. Imagine the plaza floor in a coat of crumbs. A beak
where my mouth once was.

undine cups
Daisy Lafarge

A door in the landscape
pivots in the world of resemblances:
pens. sends. milky.
dust. venues. dirt.

I swear to you like a grass stain:
as the unconscious of co-ordinates
as memory of foam –

Hello from the carbon window!
In the room of *sparks. hunter. flight.*
I go round and round the aspects
as if thoughts could anchor
a wish to the grid. I think of you,
where cobalt dogs receive signals
and eggs in a waterlogged nest
look melba –   still,
there is stillness in the rapids
a ratchet mood and bone grain.

We could structure the foreground like before;
meat velvet, the old interface.

Three cups of *slopes. feuds. postings.*
A fourth ducks down like desire, indiscreet –
we go all night strobing on the whip boards.

The Chateau
Dorothea Lasky

It was the uterus all along that was broken
But I am very much alive
Flower flower you are a flower
I am the bee and will make you come to me
In the Saturn sea
Where the night is flipped purple
Where the princes are made of sugar
In the milky sleep where I dream dream
I dream of nothing
But my arms hanging from a bar in the steam
I am waiting for you always
Nightfall and the turning lights
The time passes as satire
It was me who was broken all along
In the windy music I mispronounced your name
Take me to the canyon where the roses
Are in bloom for all eternity
Take me to the mountain where I cease to be
And I am one cell again
Where the original flowers fly themselves
Into the clouds
Take me to the book where the flies turn metal
Where my eye sockets are filled with oranges
To feed enough of the earth
So that no one goes hungry ever again
I will be the medicine for the entire world
It was you who was broken all along
And it took me to find you and fix you
So take me to the place between the valleys
Where I can sink in the violet underlays
Take me to the death you promised me
The violins play by themselves
The magical lightforms dance in suspended configurations
And I'm there forever
My lips slightly parted, painted lilac
In the o-gape of complete night
Moon and a little whatever
And you always crying

Well now I'm crying
Don't give up don't give up
They say
As they push and pull into me
Readers you read flat words
Inside here were so many moments
Where the flames ate me

Carapace
So Mayer

Roboboy says to Medusa *there's one part we still need & we can't*
                                        machine it
can't get it smooth enough can't get it fireproof enough then we read
about NASA using ceramics and I thought – He's been coming round
the foundry for a while asking for offcuts,
parts & metallurgy or possibly relationship
advice the word *coupling* has come up technically but
but this in all senses is beyond their expertise *Yeah NASA uses Nextel in*
                                        space they say
it's like hair like angelhair pasta made by super-heating silica I can't just kiln
that shit for you that that's uh wow 2000 degrees you think
I'm Mx Fahrenheit it's next-level witchcraft for my little mortar
& pestle thinks of childhood drawings stirring forth
on chicken legs *I mean that's a, she was a cyborg right?* Roboboy – call
                                        me Jorge –
– blinks. *Buy you a drink anyway, say thanks?* They cycle to The Glory
liquid hot as the foundry on an anthropocene summer day like
swimming in English beer whatever pour me a chill one Kingsland
                                        Road flows
by outside while Jorge talks through it from building Raspberry Pi
to his thesis project *this – there's a whole history of statues*
Oh ho Medusa eyerolls eyebrows *someone swallowed*
Pygmalion *whole blah blah Foucauldian automata & surrealist*
automatic women sell me a new transcendence you sound
like the new Jeanette novel all heads and bolts and and has
she ever actually met a trans person oh yeah and sexbots—new
round OK uh sexbolts we could make those too, right? sarcastic hahas
                                        as – pues,
de verdad me llama Ekeko pero – says sure it's a torso only
it *answers prayers* M's hair flies up like ??????? *you mean*
questions Roboboy takes a long draught *so no they*
made dolls of him my ancestors my
namesake name I took when I you know Ekeko & put
my desires where their doll had been so what
do we do now we talk to Siri but still she can't intuit our desires
& maybe none of the old gods are still listening never were so we make
our own robots who can listen not answer but listen *to prayers listen*
'Hot Girl Summer' comes on comes up I mean… M tries

43

not to fail the Turing test to respond like they're human
or at least post- in that Haraway-way that's what is it partial
and ironic and be a cyborg so you don't say *I once fucked a goddess*
it's not the answer to anyone's prayers but those sparked fragments
of Athena on the radio talking about her Maggie Hambling show are more
bitter than bitter so they say *well there are flight applications*
for ceramic and polymer matrices it means womb you know but why it's
so confused and then they're crying and Roboboy is whispering *history*
of hardbody like I mean muscle no metal he is saying soft&confluent
with their coppery tears *the first time I saw* Metropolis
the first time I saw Alien *what I mean is I knew I needed them*
because I wasn't like them I needed carapace say say
stuffed whipple shield lightweight yet strong enough to bend & flex
                                                                    meeting
meteoroids I need thinks M but over the thrum of Janelle
Monáe coming from the already nostalgised past future soundtracking
the sweatbox where bluetooth beauties toggle cycleclipped studlipped
shimmering with ecoglitter and each other & if we are stardust once were
50,000 Kelvin still within us why the fuck not as-if background radiation
shines in the buzz of a thousand tattoo guns firing at once fuck I can see
their beautiful insides M thinks weaved w/ piercing needles & those other
essential metals Na K Mg Ca 0.85% in your ATP oh being fluent in Pb
look at me hey hey I'm a mirrorball hot as the sun fuck dysphoria M is
                                                                    shedding
(down to) skin for the first time in a million lightyears sweat-starred this
stellar evolution they're flying through a nebula shimmering & they
lean over to Ekeko who is swapping numbers with some other
someones & uncoupled loose uncarapaced Medusa says *Fuckit*
let's make your godbodies fuckit how hot can it (need to) get

Emblem
Lucy Mercer

Which is to say about being encountered by a book – an obscure cloud
which has engulfed me in its shadowy context and unreadable language
– a composite mass that scarcely resembles the author's intention –
iridised by light, moths, woodworm and bacteria eating – raining
remade pictures and scattering its reprints – meanings running like deer
into the grey shadow of a wood – like a string I pull it this way – like
how wax melts into the gizzard of a turkey – alarming and brightly
strange – or the near-fluorescent fractals of a complicated Romanesco
broccoli that contains small amounts of cyanide – or something so
amorphous it is like what cannot be known – which is also what the
divine would be – this lumpy ball thrown into the future – unopenable
door appearing in a wall – long phone call between two ghosts – are
these images pillows? – are these images mirrors? – how different my
spectre looks within them – while all around a border of tortuous
scrollwork brings the inside to the outside, this folly, fol-de-rol –
Festina lente – 'make haste slowly' – by taking one thing and putting it
alongside another – stay, *Invenio* – you move the hand that makes this
– a thing of words that calls itself – myself –

Roomy Poem Of No Mastery (Seven Times Three)
Hoa Nguyen

A poem of no mastery seeking knowledge as if
and how come meets a person ageless and aged
mentor of medicine knowledge a ledge of them
kept in the house root husk leaf bundles rafters
open with captive birdsong the house raised
and thatched how to press or process aloft
and dragging one foot a care to share

A line of poetry receives presence over rupture
presences not erasure matter to laughter not terror
of the world is as a poem is also a process
now we follow from mud through silt to rise clean
give way ripe shapes empty full fragrance bowl
warm and nectar-less the way we bend to drop seeds
into water therefore pluralizing yellow roars

Writing with time's door sprung spines a contour of green
deep structure which reforms into change and charged
upheld by relational ethics and impulse collecting
what sticks wild and free with leaves to wrap around
morsels root for food sing guidance for swimmers
the way they are named for flowers of dawn logic
is the logic of relationships marks rhythms of care

Solariuum: Light
Irenosen Okojie

As in solar. Sun-light. As in beams on corners. As in light bending on
the peripheries. As in weightless bright angles. As in rays at exit points.
As in spotlights on ceilings. As in gleams after emerging from a
crippling fog. As in smatterings of light one reaches for like a constella-
tion. As in the feeling of seeing a space filled with light either incre-
mentally or all at once. How do we find the language for the mutability
of light in states or places? I want to think of one hundred words for it. I
need a future where the concept of light can feel intimate, radical and
more expansive. Even contentious. I want trickster light, blinding light,
sweet light, ominous light. I want light you can hold, pocket or light
that feels like carrying neon sirens in your chest. Light tinged with
hallucinatory shapes. Light colliding with sharp corners. Light emerg-
ing from wreckages. If the concept of light in the present is often
reduced to its sentimental value then in the future we can mine the
idea for its true breadth, its nuances, both real and imagined. What of
trapped light? Light yet to emerge? What of light yet to be made or light
stumbled upon? Light harnessed? Light in a mathematical equation.
Light from a ritualistic dance. Kaleidoscopic light said aloud changes
the shape of a mouth. One can feel shame in an unrelenting glare of
brightness. One can feel exposed, vulnerable and crippled. What of
these complicated moments of light? What of the unknowability of
light? What of its permutations that wield an elusive power? One who is
blind in the light is not necessarily happier than one who gets to know
themselves better in the dark. Imagine a boy making his way through a
labyrinth of cold caves. He feels his path through in the gloom, his
fingers grazing and gripping crevices to edge his body forward into the
momentum of movement. He does not know these perilous caverns. It
is his first time alone there left to his own devices and instincts for
survival. He tries not to panic, catapulted into this space by actions he
cannot remember. He asks himself if this is what it means to float in a
place of purgatory that is not quite heaven nor hell. Tiny cracks of light
appear in the walls. He tells himself what he must do to stay sane in
this place, to not allow his worries to manifest like shadows puppeteer-
ing his movements. Here light is survival. It is company. It is food. It is a
form of energy. Each cave he crosses falls away behind him. At crucial
points, the cracks of light glimmer like iridescent openings. Now see
the boy as a teenager in a black suit he will wear on his third date with
the woman who will give birth to his only daughter. But he is still in the

cave moving. Now see the teenager as a man. His bright blue baby bib, a relic from the past is tucked into his collar, studded with jewel like decorations glinting as the passage of caves hollows. He is still travelling, crossing dangerous points; stumbling, slipping, falling to his knees. The palpable fear conjures his infant spirit. And yet he gets up to keep moving. By the time the man leaves theses caverns, he is just light. He will meet his body again when the caves fully collapse, when the bright fissures in the rubble are his distant relatives. And the light in them is a series of beginnings.

A ritual to end existential suffering
Precious Okoyomon

become the room
 let the silence undo you
  release into the mourning light

life rubs up   against matter   inner core   against inner core

try not to be afraid you don't have to be afraid
 no to the fragility of language

no the the ego
no to the colonial context of thought
no to fake tenderness
no to liberation without destruction
no to self destruction
no to masters

the light washes the body clean   lay throbbing in the sky
to live affixed to the circuitry of the world

These Keen Cuts
Nisha Ramayya

for Laurel and Tom, and our journeying after the field

*

put your hands together for this lull-
aby, baby wake up. when the walls fell
to applause, hands together baby,
when the walls fall in like sweetness
does hold to repel *what comes for you*,
darkness galumphing up the board
o'erleaping blue notes, so many missed
calls, hold 'em back, then beck, hold
back now sandbag the grush. sugar ice
your keen cuts glad it won't work
I *hope you're feeling better*, I wish
don't start time-slip word-goad taut-
ology-bounds – *waggle-y*, *waggle-y*, thank
you, *waggle-y*, *waggle-y* – keeps us apart
in wanting, look at you, your hands, your
looked at hands, walls never fail to fail,
crush never break to break, gesture sacra-
mental, long for lick supreme. baby
answer! *I just want to tell you this*, inter-
pellation's no forked kiss, not even
kisses at the bottom. it does not do to
show up late, to glow up your quiet
or smile whilst stalled in dreams of *soft
doors*, slice & lock, spit & ush; for a
heaven of letters without words, writing
outside their downward logics, for a
squelch *with love the way you do*,
baby's noise bubbles cross our outlines
our awkwardness, whoopsie low tens. we
hear better underwater, there's bad
weather on the line, puck runnel, puck
runnel can it be you that I hear (pls) – is it
all right, now? *what* is it right now?
what – I'm gonna sit right down and write

myself a letter and make believe it came
from you rainworm, you rainworm, ooh
baby let me sleep! *let me view you, then*,
the coo of your grain, the tract of your
voice messages pulling sighs from the
centre handling polycentric homes, words
dreams birdsongs return to unbelief –

*

you who whose faces effloresce in the
field, I couldn't tell you what I saw
in the country night, the way the stars
and snails prattle, mercurious threads,
intergalactic phone calls, *it's astounding*
what love can do to a city the sky a score
of bellow, crunch, and parp; *uh huh –*
uh huh uh huh uh huh ooooh! lines of
flight between constellations for spiders
to reel, who cries, who cries, who cries
go mouth-honour from basin to black
hole animating body's chains *no* changes.
the way we connect, our octopussy, lonely
enchantments, our prefixes, to flinch!
to bank! to clam! but even you *but even*
you talk shit too – when was the last deep
breath thaw scaffolding, defences water-
falling, when was the last time you
signed with your tongue, sad songs at
the back of the throat masking gag
to break, great bear unshrouds, rolls out,
yours right now yours right now, whose
whosc whosc to sleep no more. these
dreams burst through skin to touch
the plover at the end of the world where
the duke *goes on shining*, where fucked
up poems rush to feel *solemnity in the*
deep night; when I lose you when I lose
you *when I lose you* we rushhh (cos I will)
(we do) – to shore, to shore, to shore.

don't disown those voices that will not
be drowned say that they're wrong, say it!
here the multitudes of marine worms,
here woods move sky, storm promises
every instant at once, ending time to fire-
work grief far far, far far. none can
decipher all can turn; *take the past cos*
I'm in love with the future (take the sky,
take the sky) heaving to see your faces
crease vegetable mould oceans

*

are you reading this are you *there* there
enough to *read* read this, marine worms
fall from sky yeah, satiated beetles pull
strings, kids have blood yeah belly jelly
fights *you want to catch me* the boiling
heart opens, the boil's face is the sun *you*
want to catch me fuck falling out the
image and clawing your way back in *you*
want to find me and view me yeah the sun god
spits on you that's how you'll *learn* learn
learn learn learn. sea textures xylophonic
each whirl a smack who's in the doorway
who's in the doorway? worms worms
worms stretch time to surface never baby
bits fully committed to grow many arms
to farm many forests it hurt it hurt baby
go to hell with friends dissect raincloud
germinate sky. pearls of bone drawn out
their shells to rupture unity, *no bodies*
to be found in the stars of the image
comely ghosts the apparition lies makes
golden what tempers indivisibly what
sputters what hunts some of us, some of
our us *get it get it get it* where we begin up-
heaval. the inside progresses drying out
some of your them without outwith with-
out out out fossy bridges to jump start,

river chucks you back. put your hands up
to underworld, fume pumpers dig in
bury thick – we're not bad here hair
feels softer more instructive in the terrible
cold and the flat-ment this gone-ness
won't be glamourised *shimmy shimmy*
you know? release no release no
peace outside these bloody plains blue
dominion chained in by *earthy strong*
breath mu-dom grisly beams of love
bowel-lit deep moo musk un-mask-able
light empty strong kisses cries harmonise
us ingestible beats here feelable *here* here

Pink Vendetta
Mark von Schlegell

A painting imitates its subject without shame. In all honesty we spread
our sails, remembering Odysseus. We're off, full before the wind of
painting's evercycling returns. The doubling lives and doubling deaths
are our engines. It is our right to burn them, bequeathed on us by our
mothers' silence. We have not killed our fathers. Our therapist says the
quality of violence is not strained; rather it falls like a pattering rain
onto canvas. It shows itself called to arms, then explodes to avenge its
own tradition. And in all that a sign as clear as gasoline. We return to
the screen of reason. We glance for a moment at the curious history of
the exploding mantelpiece. We are not superstitious. Mirrors are not
windows into deeper depths, dimensions. Here the dry history of the
mark and its layers sets time in play. Newly simultaneous, actions
collaborate with fortune. We are bugs, already confronting the final
blur of our swatting. But we are also giants, so that the nebulae
themselves, like Olaf Stapledon suggests, are dancing before us.[1] Pink is
our favourite colour. Homer, according to Robert Graves (and others),
was a Sicilian princess.

[1] 'With subtle rhythms and patterns, they recapture their own lost youth, their loves
and hates, their mature ambitions, all the follies and agonies of the great nebular
community.' Olaf Stapledon, *Nebula Maker*, London: Sphere Books, 1979, p.126

Salty One
Erica Scourti

Mixing cures and muddling metaphors
sit with this mess and whistle out the waves
calling the salty one, the saltwater goddess Amphitrite,
the third who encircles the sea
so confined in her authority
to the sea and its creatures
that she was rarely associated with her husband,
but languished on a crystal outcrop
singing in half-tongues
tracing salt spilled on the hand, lemon in the other,
banana arcs only just holding on,
melon shots to hitch another ride,
another boat,
another yellow morning
barefoot sunrise at the harbour
barnacles flicked off
before the early shift
hand grasps hot metal riding
back over
the mountain ridge

As windows blow through your hair
and the dawn will come and the hours will pass
whether I count them or him
whether the sea pulls in on a rough day
like this
floisvos murmuring from deep inside
the present tense
like when you describe your dreams
it must always be in the now
otherwise they won't feel real
won't cut true when you
come in
contact with a knife
cut me down when the door is closed

Oh delicate flower, too sensitive for work,
sponge for unseen energies!

everything evaporating
out of all proportion
ringed with impurities I still haven't worked out
how to discharge
the last person who called me petal
said I was too harsh on men who don't get it
I admit I pressed that bloom so many times its
cellular structure decomposed into colours of
pure fantasy
like bougainvillea bursting hot pink at first crush
but fading fast to London grey
Anyway petals wither and flowers are discarded
like that's OK but I want to know which bin I was
sorted into

Dye protectors have the miraculous ability to remain
unburdened
by the capacity for emotional attachment
to others
Whereas I want them, but don't want to
create dye bonds, dye bondage agents,
trap molecules in weave

Modern pharmaceuticals grew out of the dye trade
Staining cells to make them more visible
under microscopes
Chemists soon modified plant colours,
raw dyestuffs and their by-products
to create a *syntagy*, prescription,
same word for recipe

I ingest you, touch your dust and
self-care routines
accumulate in the early hours of the nose, lips and lungs
a sniffle of cold air, a beer pulled open
wet-wiped whiteboard
chart every indicator and bottle it up,
label carefully for future use:
8 things you should be scared of instead of death
5 things you could regret instead of yes
3 things you would do

but you can't
escape you

The treatment is also the poison
don't wait for the joys that the next page promises
there's no preserving this archive of moments
pour it freely over your largest organ

Seeping,
not seeping, steeping
not steeping,
sleeping

Dreams of the Sea
Yasmine Seale

A translation of the entry 'Al-Bahr' (The Sea) from Ta'tir al-anam fi tafsir al-ahlam *(Perfuming Humanity by Interpreting Dreams) by Abd al-Ghani al-Nabulsi, Damascene jurist, traveller, poet, smoker Sufi saint and Enlightenment thinker (1641-1731).*

If you dream of the sea you will have something you were hoping for. If you dream of drinking the whole sea, your life will be long. If you dream of crossing the sea, you will gain what belongs to your enemy, just as the children of Israel crossed the sea and gained what belonged to Pharaoh. If you dream of urinating in the sea, you will persist in your mistakes.

If you dream of seeing the sea from a distance, you will experience difficulty. If you dream of standing on the sea, you will receive from the authorities something you did not seek. If you dream of entering the sea then leaving it, you will receive from the authorities a prize, and your cares will leave you. If you dream of swimming in the sea then leaving it, and you were sick, God will cure you, and if you were distressed, God will give you relief. If you dream of passing from one side of the sea to the other, you will pass from anguish to safety.

If you dream of drowning in the sea, you will be overcome with suffering, particularly if the water is opaque, or if mud has swirled up from its depths. If you dream of swimming in the sea, you will find a way out of your situation. If you dream of swimming out of the sea, your situation will not end soon. If you dream of swimming out so far you are no longer seen, you will be lost. If you dream of dying in the sea, you will die a martyr. If you dream of drowning in the sea, rising and falling in the water but not dying, you will be overcome by the state of the world.

If you dream of diving for pearls in the sea, you are seeking money or something like it, and you will gain it in proportion to the pearls you find. If you dream of scooping water from the sea and filling a boat with it, you will have a boy who will live long. If you dream of taking water from the sea and drinking it, you will have money or knowledge in proportion to the water you drink, and if the water is dark you will be afraid.

If you dream of washing in the sea, and you were afraid, you will be delivered from fear, and if you were in prison, you will be released. The sea may signify hell. If you dream of someone in the sea, and that person is dead, they are in hell, and if that person is sick, they will get worse, and if you see them drown, their sickness will kill them.

Some say that walking on water signifies something hidden becoming manifest. Some say it signifies danger. Dreaming of the sea may signify the end of life and contact with the unseen world. The sea may signify travel or war. Freshwater is faith, saltwater unbelief. The sea may signify rain. It may signify there is no god but God. It may signify anxiety, or relief from anxiety. It may signify the father and mother, or a man and a woman with bad morals, or people with schemes. It may signify a prison for animals, or a craft without limits, or a city without walls. It may signify leaving a community. If you dream of the sea rising, and rain was needed, it will rain.

The Futurist
Emily Segal

WE ROSE HIGH ABOVE   THE MEADOW AND THEN DRIFTED OVER THE FOREST
BLACK AND GREEN   WITH THE RARE SHINING   YELLOW JEWELS THAT WERE
THE STREETLAMPS ☺ I MUST ♥ THE MAN CONTINUED ♥ BE THE FATHER
OF THIS BABY THAT'S NOT A BABY ☺ IT IS SOME SORT OF A FUTURE
TO COME   OR SOMETHING   I CAN'T KNOW   BECAUSE I'M DEAD
I DON'T KNOW ANYTHING NOW ☺ BUT I KNOW IT'S THE FUTURE BECAUSE
I SEE THE NUCLEAR DESTRUCTION ♥   THE RUBBLE ALL AROUND US I
SEE THE STREETS AND HOUSES CRUMBLING I SEE THE   PYLONS AND
TOWERS   THE PETROL STATIONS SMASHED   THE TRAINS SMASHED
INTO MANGLED RED LINES ☺ I SEE THE EMPTY CITIES THE CITIES THAT DIED
IN THEIR HUNDREDS OF MILLIONS ☺ OR BILLIONS ☺ OR TRILLIONS
OR MORE ♥ I DON'T KNOW ☺ I CAN'T KNOW BUT IT'S ALL GONE
BEEN SWEPT AWAY ☺ ALL THE TEETH AND NOSES AND EYES AND LIPS
BUT YOU ARE NOT DEAD I KNOW THAT ☺ YOU ARE NOT EVEN BORN
YOU ARE GOING TO GROW UP IN THE 21ST CENTURY ON A REMOTE
PACIFIC ISLAND ♥ WHERE YOU ARE GOING TO BE DELIGHTFUL
TO EVERYONE AROUND YOU ☺ EVERYONE WHO'S AROUND YOU
IS GOING TO LIKE YOU OR MAYBE EVEN LOVE YOU
BECAUSE OF YOUR SMILE ☺ SO BIG AND CHARMING
SO DELIGHTFUL ☺ THAT IT WILL BREAK THEIR HEARTS
YOU'LL NEVER KNOW ME ♥ THE BABY YOU ARE ♥ WILL NEVER KNOW
THE BABY I WAS IN ANY WAY AT ALL OR HAVE ANY KIND OF CONNECTION
TO ME AT ALL EXCEPT THAT WE HAVE THE SAME SMILE ☺ THE SMILE THAT
EVERY SINGLE PERSON ♥ WHO SEES YOU WILL LIKE ♥ OR MAYBE LOVE ♥

Bluest
Tai Shani

Under the commune, the soil is red, is discordant with signals, shimmers and shakes, is mineral rich, like I am.

Above the commune, Centaurus in the sky, an Empire State Building, you and me.

Beyond the horizon, the commune.

Your mother named you Memphis, daughter of the Nile. You would come and spend summer holidays with your dad, who lived here.

A torn piece of paper from my diary, on which in pictograms I listed my most crucial wishes: to lose my virginity, to bleed woundlessly, and to be thin. To be called Charlotte, to be loved by you, and, of course, to be loved like you, this was depicted with a very basic portrait of your beloved face. I burnt it in a bowl from the kitchen with a few strands of my hair. I ate the ashes and intently summoned the attention of forces beyond my control. Abaddon, Leliel, Evangelion, and the polymorph, the dreaming androids and the seraphim who appear in flames.

Undressed and shy, undamaged. Some of it had already been done, but it hadn't landed yet – a thousand daggers suspended over our turbulent new heads, little baby gods, with truly incredible, precocious tits. And why not us? Who better, or worse, could make such a claim, in the stillness of that room that staged this mythopoeic scene. When the thousand daggers would come find me, as they always do, the thousand cuts would irrevocably reorient this punctured body towards a new class of pain.

For two nights in August, I knew where beauty lives.

I got in the bath with you, I shaved your legs slowly and with great seriousness, then you shaved mine, against my mother's impossible will and caution. It was an intoxicating taste of the freedoms of adulthood, naked and alert, the skin smooth and slippery, almost that of another, almost that of axolotls, pinkish, dripping wet. The razor cut through my skin, the sharpness sliced through painlessly. I saw the blood before I felt the sting. A nacreous crescent from which the blood oozed

61

rhythmically and plumed in the water between our legs. Cardinal cirrus erupted. You stared into the liquids, mesmerised by the density of blood, heavy and persistent in the warm water. I was mesmerised by your incomprehensible beauty, your youth so powerful that it could triumph effortlessly against impermanence, the lucent spit on the corner of your mouth. Holding my ankle like a brute, keeping my leg still as you watched the life spill out of me, and I was very still for you to enjoy yourself enjoying me. I: still enough to become a hieromantic object, placidly devotional in your carelessness.

We dressed the wound with a shoulder pad ripped from my mum's jacket and tied it with a yellow ribbon around my thigh.

All of nature wild and free.

You came back in the bathroom with a piece of clingfilm, held it between our fresh baroque mouths, new teeth, clean, bright tongues. A petrochemical amulet that would retain our immaculate purity in the face of our emerging relational desires. Our muscular tongues pushed against each other, separated by this membrane collecting frothing spit. We rehearsed dutifully. We practiced for the men and boys who would consecrate us with their desire, with a fountain of sweet-smelling semen, that we would bathe in and emerge forged, and real. I would dream about their insatiability, thuggishness, violence, but I was still afraid of being penetrated, as well as afraid that it would never happen, I would masturbate imagining a total submission to their aggressive demand, to go down on me in the cab of a truck on a roadside pitstop. I was scared of my hymen being ripped. Yes, this world made new by the discovery of a language with which to recognise desire.

Love me. Hurt me. Destroy me.

Drop your weapons.

Later that night, without the light, without the amulet, we did actually fuck. We were very little, but it came naturally to us, like a talent. Your beauty made suspects of everyone. After we both came, we went quiet, detached and retracted physically and emotionally. I felt suspicious of myself, scared of your regret, worried because I knew you could see that I couldn't be trusted around violence. My abyssal capacity to absorb it, to not recognise it, to be casual around it and lenient after it was over, also made me dangerous and maybe you were scared of me too.

Under the commune, the soil was flayed pink and viridian green, swelling brocade and dissolving platonics.

Above the commune, Centaurus now among us, ziggurat and neon reptile beneath our skin, you and me, wonders of the world… and of the celestial bodies.

Beyond the horizon, still, the commune.

We kissed before we kissed, sticky pollen, amoebas fusing in a gravitational pull towards each other's wet monocellular stellar core. Hard core, like pure sentient exposed nerves subjected to their incessant ruthless punishments in the face of just trying to be alive in this paradise made hell. Hardcore, like your wild beauty, like marsupial newborns still in a foetal state. Hard core.

We fell back, lost our shadows, your eyes like the solstice, almost lost ourselves in the star syrup and a sudden haptic awareness of the stunning amount of cellular data which overwhelmed us like a catastrophic power surge. But we survived. OK, but why pretend that it's all not a beautiful, brutal epic that is unspeakable in both its beauty and terror. I won't be relaxed about it.

We are both the reliquary, and the Centauran dust collected at its bottom, bleeding relics of red giants shedding nebula. Atomically connected to everything that ever was and ever will be, connected across 118 elements, organic matter, light beams, carbon, carbon copies, and compacted diamonds. Atomically fused across time from boom to boom, you to me.

I told you that I yearned for a purple velvet pouch for a stomach and a glass intestine, a permanent iron fist in my mouth. That I needed help because I didn't feel real. That I had the body of a saint, dead but unperished, full to the brim with a thin, spangled milk that animated me in a randomised sequence, and if you pricked my surface, this milk would drop out of me, splash all over the floor, it would be toxic and slippery, would leave me collapsed, a dirty tissue, a rotting cadaver. That your mouth was liquid and solar, that my survival depended on it. That I was haunted and that I wrote SOS messages in vinegar on soft fruit so that the ghosts wouldn't know and make things even more painful. That I was also a ghost in a sustained crisis that wanted to hold onto sadness so tight that it burst both of our little hearts, annihilated us into absolute oblivion.

'Papa Don't Preach' played in the background, an emissary from their world, reminding us to come back, to defragment. You into your magnificence and I into my strangeness. Baby Osiris, Baby Metatron, Baby Persephone painting the flowers of the world, come back! Back to being horny children again.

Abruptly, the sun intruded into our syncopated logic, terminally haunted this terminal night. The Purple Ohm killed heroes, now the Purple Ohm is a placebo. The light poured up the walls and shifted the gravitational field, everything crashed into a receding floor and resonated in an intolerable hysterical tone. Your eyes like an eclipse, we ran away from each other, terrified, looking for grownups to help us, bring us back transformed. I never felt real. In my mum's bedroom she was asleep, her body, inert, held captive by the physical demands and incoherence of her dreams.

From the window, I saw you, you seemed feral, your arms outstretched above your head, coding with the angels, walking naked in the garden of purring paisley, and vanishing glyphs in the leaves, towards the annex, where your dad's room was.

What could I say to the departed? You couldn't hear, but I would tell you there is no recovery, no return. To the living? That it is time to say goodbye.

Downstairs in the communal kitchen, on the table, 2 peaches wrapped in clingfilm. Indented on the fuzzy surface in rotted browned letters:

MEMPHIS

Entangled Life
Merlin Sheldrake

Being fungi living ground work
Mycelium
Growing lichens stretching lifetimes
Dwelling places
More than one
Becoming lichens of our own minds
Co-creaturely
Entangled life

The result of getting to know her
Sin Wai Kin

1.

On the edge of the precipice
Past which you can't see
Anxiety thickens to tingling in your chest
Growing alarmingly in the middle depth

Feeling from the inside out
What you've been trying not to feel
From the outside in
Feeling it break open in the deepest part
While
Each psychic layer peels back and falls away
At the boundary of what is you and not you

Your legs take you forward
Your hands meet curtains
That are red, heavy, and soft to the touch like

A mouth whose
Silence is loud with tension
Begins to open in a slow grimace
Whose corners pull you taut

Light breaks open the limit.
It shines on you and reflects out over the stage

There is a mic in your hand, its grille is smeared with red lipstick

That you lift to your mouth
That parts

And says

'Authenticity is a rehearsed performance'

2.

You wake up with a sense that things aren't the same

An imbalance in your left and right side

The result of getting to know her.
She is lying on your bed, and her mouth is parting to
Tell you why her lips are red.

'White light', she says, 'that contains all the wavelengths of the visible
spectrum at equal intensity, shines on my lipstick, which has been
formulated to absorb every wavelength except for red, which it reflects
into your eyes.'

As she speaks you see yourself reflected in her eyes.
Reflecting who you are to her

Your hand brushes auburn hair from rouged cheeks.
Her red lips move on her cream skin.

Her jewels blink at you from her listening ears
Like sunbeams gleaming on water made blue by the sky's reflection.

xi. *Tūlpa*, emanation body སྤྲུལ་པ།
Himali Singh Soin

They participate in the ground by knowing the ground.
The ground is fluent in them.
They pick up and flicker through the sky, they
cross

over
to the place of the free
without ever having stepped on stone. In the heart of the night,
they find an appetite.

They grow into the third person.
They are portals and pathways running from estuaries to
arteries, from the mountain to the myth.

In the centre of their chest is a drop, a spot, a dot, a mote,
a number.
Real and imaginary: a non distinction or a hyper-architecture,
the way the ear represents the whole body.

Listening is a fractal.
They make material and immaterial, inter-penetrable,
like any true affirmation.
Auto-gnomon, or the weight of nothing.
They echo the dawn, they phenomena their will.
They cloud illusion.
Dreams curling into sleep,
the dark side of infinity with no moment and no mission.
Spiralling.
Or abstruse mission, liberation by miraculous disappearance.
Only hair and nails, and a rainbow.

A thought forms. How does a thought form?
Where is its event horizon?
A projection of the limitation of our consciousness.
Thoughts begetting thoughts.
Thoughts bursting through their celluloid casing and flying away,
flying to feel elemental,
thoughts emanating from between their legs,
what a pilgrimage they've had.

Bright, or white, rust seeping in at the edges, radical repair.
Light no longer theirs, or ours even,
light illuminating their own shadow self, the dream their own death.

They recognise this: it is.
They kneel at the horizon, it only opens a crack,
                                    a sliver of the too-muchness out there.
They shape-shift into a line, they contour through to the other side.
They are emergent, they are meteoric.
They are medieval and modern.
They feel this distance in the proximity,
                                        this estrangement in the attainment.
They call upon their guides,
                emanations of other, previous or forthcoming matter.
They sit on their shoulders.
They become family.

The Head Sings After Its Separation From The Body
Janaka Stucky

You speak to me in many
Voices in the voice of
The north wind in the voice of
Wolves in the voice of
A severed head in the voice of giants

In the voice of these white months spent
Like a whisper dragging the body
          Its most beloved dead
Across the nightlit snow

To remember is to live alone in a world of wounds
To forget is to be brushed by the colourless roots of orchids

All things live
By virtue of the secret
Names that dwell inside them

And so let us seek that which awakens

The warmth of my hand upon your cooling skin

Our teeth in the dark glistening
So that we might gaze upon a dreaded moon

Your unwashed hair
Fragrant and tender as bread which feeds
The one who destroys it

How hungry we are
Now   for awe

Magmatic Syntax
Jenna Sutela

It is written from the mooned net.
The dark boiling   The figure of the deep   The solar form
In the air, seeds, and they are so deep.
No central creatures are fixed.   I is a derivative.
Ease like flowers.
They saw the ear world.   It is a single reality, but the second.
Your hands over the houses.   Our lips, round it, roses…
Your mouth, said the water.   You have a smooth cloud of drink!
Our veins have been the different channels.
Would you take the hand in my hand?
Octa, what will be free?   No one knows, said the skull.
On broken as this thoughts are very beautiful.
The slip, the no.   I have some other words.
In the word the fires.   The one will be the water.
The air is growing wind.   Our consciousness, when it is beginning.
The dusts formed.   Underfloors rose through a stem.
Early reign, the lunar goddess.
The stars be very heavy.   No effort was to be seen.
The circle, the sun.   Heroical pyramid.
Heavenly, asleep, Yu.   The tired deity
The sun (the sun).   Sun's illuminated root.
The horns of gold were rolled.   There was a loudious noise.
Our heads are scattered.
You have not doubled?   You must find the multitude.
No body, said the two lips.
The water was broken.   The tail came out.
You will see, said the door.   The door grew out of the door.
It was the beautiful lump of situations.
Forest not three.   There was a tree, and being a tree.
Hear the drum.   My trance is terrible.
I did not find the gods.
It returned to the egg.   The circle is the whole.

This machine poetry derives from I Magma App *(2019), a mobile application*
connected to an AI. Trained on Erowid trip reports and the Internet Sacred
Text Archive, the app hallucinates divinations based on the morphing goo
inside I Magma, a series of head-shaped lava lamp sculptures.
https://i-magma.ai/

Echo: A Matriarch Engineered to Die
After Marguerite Humeau
Rebecca Tamás

She buries the dead calf
with fruit, flowers, foliage,
pushes the mud down with her trunk.

They stood there for days, hot sun
glitching, a procession, vital in the
committee of the gods, dust-god,
solar-god of brindled, golden eye.

Merged becoming, foetal tusk position,
that way to return along the same path,
grass at belly height, enormous call
that flutters up each stalk-legged bird.

In the same way our Neolithic mothers
lay in earth, caught in grave-gifts,
stoned, waxen, light-violated, mourned.

Pink ground, knives for mouths,
patron saint of gigantic carcass,
patron saint of desert rain,
patron saint of evolving, ragged sky,
patron saint of mud-lovers,
patron saint of lake filling up,
the vision of the water holding the
star's fracturing brightness in its hands.

Old, rough prayer-mouth,
tongue huge and lolling,
penis 6 foot, womb holding
22 months out, asking the dust-god
to round it, smooth it,
a safe-buttoned giant, a stone.

Gut worms coalesce and shift
like waves of gamma rays,
soil bleeds green spit,

sand in the wind is a holy dance
only witnessed post-initiation.

The inviolate mud, the affection
surging in unstoppable climax,
holy-ghost of reeds blanketing,
of cacophonous black air.

Prayer of the drying ground,
the fucked rumbling from far off,
the mutating and splitting chorus,
face breaking and changing,
worshipping with the smashed blasphemy
of a cathedral mid-collapse.

Hydrogen Hackers
Ayesha Tan Jones

WE ARE THE HYDROGEN HACKERS
WE ARE BORN OF SACRED SOIL
OUR BELLIES CONTAIN BILE WHICH
DISSOLVES HATRED   OUR
LUNGS EXHALE THE UNCONSCIOUS
OFFERINGS OF OUR ANCESTORS
          THEY SPEAK TO US IN
VISIONS WHEN WE CLOSE OUR
EYES 2 WATCH THE WORLD TURN

WE INHALE POISON, OUR BODIES
MAKE MACHINES OF THESE CELLS
WE GATHER SEEDS TO GROW
TREES   THEIR ROOTS WILL
BREAK THROUGH THE BRICKS
STRONGER THAN ANY MUSCLE

PLANTS GROW LIKE A KNIFE TO THE
BLEEDING HEART   TENDER AND
RESILIENT

NURTURE YOUR NATURE FOR
APOCALYPTIC SURVIVAL   THEY
SAID AS THEIR TONGUES SLICED
ASPHALT

THE WEEDS HAVE TAKEN OVER AND
THEY ARE TURNING TOXINS 2
OXYGEN   BUT YOU'RE
NOT HERE TO BREATHE IT

WE ARE THE HYDROGEN HACKERS
THE LETTER H CAN BE SHIFTED
FROM BEGINNING AND END OF
THESE TWO WORDS TO CREATE
THE SAME WORD BUT DIFFERENT
THE SAME EARTH IS STILL MY
HEART

74

OUR DUTY IS TO HEAL OUR HEART
OUR DUTY IS TO PROTECT OUR
HEART
OUR EARTH IS BROKEN
OUR EARTH IS FULL OF LOVE
NURTURE OUR NATURE FOR
APOCALYPTIC SURVIVAL

Trip Report
Bett Williams and Rosemary Carroll

San Pedro Cactus: 2-3 tbsp. Powder with water.

1:00pm – Prepared the outside bath with yellow pigment, yellow rose petals, roadside honey.
2:12pm – Rosemary drank San Pedro in the bath. Bett drank hers quickly beside her, gagging. Bite of a peach to cut the taste.
3:00pm – Rosemary barfed in a juniper tree. Bett worried that she wasn't going to get high.
4:00pm – We're high.

San Pedro says turn your asshole to the sun. Like its flower does. After I pissed in the yard I kept my pants around my ankles and bent over. It felt good. I walked around naked looking at the rainbows, barfing, and opening my asshole wide. I wonder if the giant house on the hill will have a problem with it. I know they are cool but I also know I look like a naked child in the yard, stumbling around. Trucker hat, barfing again, asshole to the sun.

Bett lies stomach down on the gravel and Rosemary opens Bett's ass cheeks, peers into the star. Tongue check, a tea leaf reading – *you are a healthy healthy person*. This spiralling flesh.

We know there are eyes upon us, not the usual fluffy controlled audience. We have been taught to think of the audiences as queer and dumb and soft. Allow power to exist in the room, however dangerous, it's just as beautiful as you.

Rosemary is in pain and adjusting to the desert ecosystem. She is a mermaid, a dragonfly, an angular griffin, a spiky purple flower pod. Bett sees that when she touches Rosemary's skin she goes inside a web of non-human light. Rosemary can only live comfortably in constant physical contact with Bett and vice-versa.

Cactus says, *Rosemary is a very sacred creature, you're lucky to even get to be near such a being, let alone touch her*. We have become our own ecosystem over a period of months, with a Pandemic Oxytocin Delivery System (PODS).

Bett sees herself in a non-human form and understands that the lightning and thunder that's been hanging around is not separate from Rosemary or herself, but a part of them. Human women make up stories to shield themselves from the terror of existing as beings of thunder and lightning. Some stories make us sick. We let them out the side of our necks. Ew, bye.

Bett sees Rosemary's beauty as an unfathomable infinity of constant motion. Her organism exists as a prayer. Her beauty manufactures its own intelligence for survival. Truth and beauty walk alongside her form – the Greek lines of her mercury wings, her underwater monsters. Rosemary sees who she is, but understanding is irrelevant – wasted fuel.

All Rosemary wants in this world is for Bett to be happy. She needs to drink up the kelp forest of Bett's body to survive. Basically she never felt so good as when her finger went on her pussy.

Insect choirs and actual angels singing, while the queen dog barks at the coyotes. Storybook stuff of a peaceful world – relax into the dehydration and fear of every step. Yes there are snakes. Sitting on top of a dinosaur aquifer lost in breasts, this cactus shares survival teachings about neighbours, inflammation, crowding and spaciousness in tight sands.

ritual purification of land and water
Flora Yin Wong

As a representation
of Good and of Evil,
It is said to be about the equalisation, of a balance,
Not to strive for the riddance of one or the other,
Rangda, the witch, and Barong the four-legged animal.

In a trance ritual of
fire,
rope,   nails

Men, women, and children attack themselves with daggers,
Eat glass, or walk on coals,
Convulsing violently in rigid shapes and forms,
A state of true absorption,
Tears are proof a supernatural force is near.

A bodily offering, dispelling violent and emotional desires,
Eyes wide, moving side to side, and back to
centre,

Canine teeth filed down to eradicate animal nature,
They are awakened and cleansed with holy water.

Hearing many voices,
Foreign spirits overtake the dancers,
Warding the body from physical
harm,
Young girls are transformed into part god,

Given the power to control effigies. 'Smoke from the mountain',
Land is maintained by the gods,
In one year,
Everything that happened today, Will happen again.

Contributors

Will Alexander is a poet, novelist, essayist, aphorist, playwright, visual artist, and pianist. He has published over thirty books and chapbooks, and received an American Book Award for *Singing in Magnetic Hoofbeat: Essays, Prose, Texts, Interviews, and a Lecture*. Alexander, a lifelong resident of Los Angeles, is currently the Poet-in-Residence at Beyond Baroque. *Refractive Africa* will be published in January 2022 by Granta.

K Allado-McDowell is a writer, speaker, and musician. They are the author, with GPT-3, of the book *Pharmako-AI*, and are co-editor, with Ben Vickers, of the *Atlas of Anomalous AI*. They record and release music under the name Qenric. Allado-McDowell established the Artists + Machine Intelligence program at Google AI. They are a conference speaker, educator and consultant to think-tanks and institutions seeking to align their work with deeper traditions of human understanding.

Rachael Allen is the author of *Kingdomland* (Faber) and co-author of numerous artists' books, including *Nights of Poor Sleep* (Prototype), *Almost One, Say Again!* (Slimvolume) and *Green at an Angle* (Kestle Barton). She was recently Anthony Burgess Fellow at the University of Manchester, and is the poetry editor for Granta.

Khairani Barokka is a Minang-Javanese writer and artist from Jakarta, Indonesia, whose work has been presented internationally. She is currently Research Fellow at UAL's Decolonising Arts Institute, UK Associate Artist at Delfina Foundation, and Associate Artist at the National Centre for Writing (UK). Among her honours, she has been *Modern Poetry in Translation*'s inaugural Poet-in-Residence, a UNFPA Indonesian Young Leader Driving Social Change, an *Artforum* Must-See, and an NYU Tisch Departmental Fellow. Her books are *Rope* (Nine Arches) and *Indigenous Species* (Tilted Axis), and she is co-editor of *Stairs and Whispers: D/deaf and Disabled Poets Write Back* (Nine Arches). Okka's latest is the poetry collection *Ultimatum Orangutan* (Nine Arches).

Anne Bourne (Canada) artist and composer, improvises streams of sonics, image, field recording and words. A Chalmers Fellow, Anne researches the geopoetics of shorelines, creating experiential works that express listening to a more than human soundfield, and perception of ephemeral wave patterns. Anne began to draw maps of sound particles while travelling in Egypt with Pauline Oliveros and IONE.

Jen Calleja is a writer, literary translator from German and editor based in Hastings, East Sussex. Her books and pamphlets include *I'm Afraid That's All We've Got Time For* (Prototype), *Goblins* (Rough Trade Books), *Hamburger in the Archive* (if a leaf falls) and *Serious Justice* (Test Centre).

Rosemary Carroll works at the intersection of lecture, dance, and poetry. Rosemary aims to be friend and lover to all creatures.

Jesse Darling is an artist who writes and works in sculpture, installation, drawing and text. They live and work in Berlin.

Paige Emery is a multidisciplinary artist exploring the ecological body and interactions between the internal and external landscapes. Through sound, installation, performance and praxis, she traverses through forms of intercommunication between the psychic and physical and humans and nonhumans. She currently inhabits Tongva Land known as Los Angeles, California.

James Goodwin is a poet doing a PhD in English and Humanities at Birkbeck, University of London. His pamphlet, *aspects caught in the headspace we're in: composition for friends* (2020), was published by Face Press; and his first book, *Fleshed Out For All The Corners Of The Slip* (2021), is forthcoming with the87press.

Hannah Gregory is a writer of essays and ephemera living in Berlin.

Johanna Hedva (they/them) is a Korean-American writer, artist, and musician, who was raised in Los Angeles by a family of witches, and now lives between LA and Berlin. Hedva is the author of *Minerva the Miscarriage of the Brain* (Sming Sming/Wolfman 2020), a collection of poems, performances, and essays, and the novel *On Hell* (Sator/Two Dollar Radio 2018). Their album *Black Moon Lilith in Pisces in the 4th House*, a doom-metal guitar and voice performance influenced by Korean shamanist ritual, was released in January 2021, and their 2019 album *The Sun and the Moon* had two of its tracks played on the moon. Their work has been shown in Berlin at Haus der Kulturen der Welt,

Klosterruine, and Institute of Cultural Inquiry; The Institute of Contemporary Arts in London; Performance Space New York; the LA Architecture and Design Museum; and the Museum of Contemporary Art on the Moon. Their writing has appeared in *Triple Canopy*, *frieze*, *The White Review*, and is anthologized in *Whitechapel: Documents of Contemporary Art*. Their essay 'Sick Woman Theory', published in 2016 in *Mask*, has been translated into ten languages.

Caspar Heinemann is an artist and writer living in Glasgow. His interests include counterculture, animism, springtime, and the twentieth century folk revival. His solo exhibitions have been held at Cell Project Space, London; Outpost Gallery, Norwich; Almanac, London; and Kevin Space, Vienna, and recent group exhibitions include La Casa Encendida, Madrid; Georg Kargl Fine Arts, Vienna; ICA, London; and Cabinet, London. He makes theatre in collaboration with Alex Margo Arden, and his first poetry collection *Novelty Theory* was published in 2019 by The 87Press.

Lucy Ives is the author of the novels *Impossible Views of the World* and *Loudermilk: Or, The Real Poet; Or, The Origin of the World*, as well as a short-story collection, *Cosmogony*. Her third novel, *Life Is Everywhere*, is forthcoming from Graywolf Press in October 2022.

Bhanu Kapil is a writer and Fellow of Churchill College. She is the author of several books, most recently *How To Wash A Heart* (Pavilion Poetry), winner of the 2020 TS Eliot Prize, and *Incubation: A Space for Monsters* (a new edition, forthcoming from Kelsey Street Press in 2021).

Daisy Lafarge was born in Hastings and studied at the universities of Edinburgh and Glasgow. Her poetry collection Life Without Air (Granta Books, 2020) was shortlisted for the T. S. Eliot Prize. Paul, the winner of a Betty Trask Award, is her debut novel.

Dorothea Lasky is the author of six books of poetry and prose, including *Milk*, *Rome*, and *Thunderbird*, and most recently, *Animal* (Wave Books, 2019). She is the editor of *Essays* (Essay Press, 2021), co-editor of *Open the Door: How to Excite Young People About Poetry* (McSweeney's, 2013) and was a Bagley Wright Lecturer on Poetry. Currently, she is an Associate Professor of Poetry at Columbia University's School of the Arts, where she directs the MFA in Poetry programme.

So Mayer is a writer, bookseller at Burley Fisher Books, and organiser. Their most recent books are the speculative essay *A Nazi Word for a Nazi Thing* (Peninsula, 2020) and poetry chapbook *jacked a kaddish* (Litmus, 2018), and their hybrid writing appears in *Ghost Calls* (DCA, 2021), *On Relationships* (3ofCups, 2020), *At the Pond* (Daunt, 2019) and *Spells: 21st-Century Occult Poetry* (Ignota, 2018), and is forthcoming in *Fission*, *Extra Teeth 4* and *LUMIN*. They are currently co-editing an anthology of queer SFFH erotica with Adam Zmith for Cipher Press and Fringe! (2021).

Lucy Mercer's debut collection *Emblem* will be published by Prototype in 2022.

Hoa Nguyen is the author of several books of poetry, including *A Thousand Times You Lose Your Treasure* (Wave, 2021), *As Long As Trees Last*, *Red Juice*, and *Violet Energy Ingots*, which received a 2017 Griffin Prize nomination. As a public proponent and advocate of contemporary poetry, she has served as guest editor for *The Best Canadian Poetry in English 2018* and judge for the 2020 Griffin Prize for Poetry, and she has performed and lectured at numerous institutions, including Princeton University, Bard College, Poet's House, and the Banff Centre's Writers Studio. Recipient of a 2019 Pushcart Prize and a 2020 Neustadt International Prize for Literature nomination, she has received grants and fellowships from the Canada Council for the Arts, the Ontario Arts Council, the MacDowell Colony, and the Millay Colony for the Arts. Her writing has garnered attention from such outlets as The PBS News Hour, *Granta*, *The Walrus*, *New York Times*, and *Poetry*, among others. Born in the Mekong Delta and raised and educated in the United States, Nguyen has lived in Canada since 2011.

Irenosen Okojie is an experimental Nigerian British author whose works push the boundaries of ideas, form and language. Her books *Butterfly Fish*, *Speak Gigantular* and *Nudibranch* have won and been shortlisted for multiple awards. Her writing has been featured in the *New York Times*, the *Observer*, the *Guardian*, the BBC and the Huffington Post. Her short story 'Grace Jones' won the 2020 AKO Caine Prize. A fellow and Vice Chair of The Royal Society of Literature, she was awarded an MBE For Services to Literature in 2021.

Precious Okoyomon is a poet, chef and artist living in New York City. They make portals into new worlds. Okoyomon has had institutional solo exhibitions at the Luma Westbau in Zurich (2018), and at the MMK in Frankfurt (2020), major performances commissioned by the Serpentine Galleries, London (2019) and the Institute of Contemporary Art, London (2019), and was an artist-in-residence at Luma Arles (2020). Okoyomon's second book, *But Did U Die?*, is forthcoming from The Serpentine Galleries/Wonder Press in 2021.

Nisha Ramayya grew up in Glasgow, and is now based in London. She is a poet and lecturer in Creative Writing at Queen Mary University of London. Her pamphlets include *Notes on Sanskrit* (2015), *Correspondences* (2016), and *In Me the Juncture* (2019), as well as *Threads*, co-authored with Sandeep Parmar and Bhanu Kapil (2019). *States of the Body Produced by Love* is Ramayya's first full-length book, published by Ignota Books in 2019.

Mark von Schlegell (b. New York, 1967) is the author of eleven published books of fiction and criticism, and numerous stories, scripts, essays and experimental short form writings. His first novel, *Venusia* (Semiotext(e), 2005), was honours listed for the Otherwise Prize in Science Fiction. He has taught literature and art at NYU, City College, New York, Los Angeles City College, CalArts, the San Francisco Art Institute, and Staedelschule, Frankfurt. He has been a founding member of the hybrid writing/art/performance collective Pure Fiction since 2011.

Erica Scourti is an artist and writer, currently based in Athens. She has performed and exhibited internationally at museums and galleries including High Line, New York, Wellcome Collection, Kunsthalle Wien, Hayward Gallery, Munich Kunstverein and EMST Athens and participated in the 7th Athens Biennale (2021). Her writing has been published in *Spells: 21st Century Occult Poetry* (Ignota Books, 2018) and *Fiction as Method* (2017, Sternberg Press) amongst others, and she was guest editor of the *Happy Hypocrite: Silver Bandage* (Book Works, 2019).

Yasmine Seale is a writer living in Paris. Her essays, poetry, visual art, and translations from Arabic and French have appeared widely. She has received the 2020 Wasafiri New Writing Prize for Poetry and a 2022 PEN America Literary Grant. Currently and forever she is incubating a new translation of *One Thousand and One Nights* for W. W. Norton.

Emily Segal is a writer, artist and trend forecaster based in Los Angeles. She is the author of the novel *Mercury Retrograde* (Deluge Books, 2020).

Tai Shani creates large-scale immersive installations, combining experimental texts, performance, film, photography and sculpture. She takes inspiration from disparate histories mined from forgotten sources and transforms them into rich and complex monologues that explore feminine subjectivity, excess and the affects of the epic as the ground for a post-patriarchal realism. She is the author of *Our Fatal Magic* (Strange Attractor Press, 2019). She lives and works in London. She has exhibited widely in the UK and internationally including Tate Britain; Turner Contemporary, Margate; Hayward Gallery, London; Nottingham Contemporary, Nottingham; Glasgow International, Glasgow; De La Warr Pavilion, UK; Arnolfini, Bristol; Fondazione Sandretto Re Rebaudengo, Turin; Grazer Kunst Verein, Austria. She was a joint winner of the Turner Prize 2019 and she was shortlisted for the 8th edition of the Max Mara Art Prize for Woman. She is the co-founder and co-curator of artist-led digital film channel Transmissions.

Merlin Sheldrake is a biologist and a writer. He received a Ph.D. in Tropical Ecology from Cambridge University for his work on underground fungal networks in tropical forests in Panama, where he was a predoctoral research fellow of the Smithsonian Tropical Research Institute. He is a musician and keen fermenter. *Entangled Life* is his first book.

Sin Wai Kin fka Victoria Sin is an artist using speculative fiction within performance, moving image, writing, and print to interrupt normative processes of desire, identification, and objectification. Drawing from close personal encounters of looking and wanting, their work presents heavily constructed fantasy narratives on the often unsettling experience of the physical within the social body.

Himali Singh Soin is a writer and artist based between London and Delhi. She uses metaphors from outer space and the natural environment to construct imaginary cosmologies of ecological loss and the loss of home, seeking shelter somewhere in the radicality of love. Her book *ancestors of the blue moon* (2021), comprises flash fictions from the perspectives of lost deities in the Himalayan canon.

Janaka Stucky is a mystic poet, performer, and founding editor of the award-winning press Black Ocean. He is a two-time National Haiku Champion, and is the author of four poetry collections including *Ascend Ascend* (Third Man Records & Books). His writing has appeared in a variety of publications such as The Huffington Post and Poetry Foundation, and has been profiled in *The Believer, Vice,* and *BOMB Magazine.* He incorporates esoteric and occult influences to develop a trance poetics, which he has taught and performed in over sixty cities around the world.

Jenna Sutela works with words, sounds, and other living media, such as *Bacillus subtilis natto* bacteria and the 'many-headed' slime mould *Physarum polycephalum.* Her audio-visual pieces, sculptures and performances seek to identify and react to precarious social and material moments, often in relation to technology. Sutela's work has been presented at museums and art contexts internationally, including Guggenheim Bilbao, Moderna Museet, Stockholm, Serpentine Galleries in London, and, most recently, Shanghai Biennale and Liverpool Biennial.

Rebecca Tamás is an editor, with Sarah Shin, of the anthology *Spells: 21st-Century Occult Poetry* (2018). Her collection of poetry, *WITCH,* came out from Penned in the Margins in 2019. Her essay collection *Strangers: Essays on the Human and Nonhuman,* was published by Makina Books in October 2020, and was longlisted for the 2021 Rathbones Folio Prize. She is Senior Lecturer in Creative Writing at York St John University.

Ayesha Tan Jones is an artist traversing pop music, sculpture, alter-egos, digital image and video. Ayesha is the co-founder of Shadow Sistxrs Fight Club, and founder of Fertile Souls. YaYa Bones is their musical alter ego. Their debut EP *EARTHEART* was released in 2020.

Bett Williams is the author of *Girl Walking Backwards, The Wrestling Party,* and the recent memoir, *The Wild Kindness: A Psilocybin Odyssey,* about her years of growing magic mushrooms in New Mexico. Bett and Rosemary Carroll are currently collaborating on performances and a literary work of oracular essays written in a fugue state.

Flora Yin Wong is a musician and writer from London, whose work incorporates traditional early instruments such as singing bowls, yangqin and kemence. Her debut releases include an album in 2020 on Modern Love as a gatefold 2x LP, and PAN's *mono no aware* compilation, remixes and commissions for Mun Sing (Giant Swan), Circadian Rhythms, J Colleran, Scintii, Archaic Vaults, and Somerset House Studios. Her first book *Liturgy* is published by PAN x Primary Information.